EARTHLIGHT

NEW MEDITATIONS FOR CHILDREN

Also by Maureen Garth

Starbright
Moonbeam
Sunshine
The Inner Garden
InnerSpace
The Power of the Inner Self

EARTHLIGHT

NEW MEDITATIONS FOR CHILDREN

Maureen Garth

HarperCollinsPublishers

HarperCollins*Publishers*

First published in Australia in 1997
Reprinted in 1998, 1999, 2000
by HarperCollins*Publishers* Pty Limited
ABN 36 009 913 517
A member of the HarperCollins*Publishers* (Australia) Pty Limited Group
http://www.harpercollins.com.au

HarperCollins*Publishers*
25 Ryde Road, Pymble, Sydney, NSW 2073, Australia
31 View Road, Glenfield, Auckland 10, New Zealand
77-85 Fulham Palace Road, London W6 8JB, United Kingdom
Hazelton Lanes, 55 Avenue Road, Suite 2900, Toronto, Ontario M5R 3L2
and 1995 Markham Road, Scarborough, Ontario M1B 5M8, Canada
10 East 53rd Street, New York NY 10022, USA

National Library of Australia Cataloguing-in-Publication data:

Garth, Maureen.
Earthlight: new meditations for children.
ISBN 0 7322 5828 6.
1. Meditation – Juvenile literature.
2. Meditations – Juvenile literature. I. Title.
158.12083

Edited by Kevin Mark Editorial and Literary Services
Cover illustration: Stella Danalis
Printed in Kong Kong by Skiva Printing and Binding Co., Ltd
on 100gsm Woodfree

9 8 7 6 5 4   00 01 02 03

For Eleanor
Who is my light
My love
My inspiration

A Note from the Publisher

After completing this manuscript, Maureen Garth discovered that she had cancer. Although she had successfully overcome cancer in the past, this was not to be the case this time. Maureen continued her speaking and teaching engagements about meditation for as long as she was able, but passed on from this life a few months before the publication of this book.

Following the release of her previous book of children's meditations, *Sunshine*, Maureen deliberately delayed writing a further children's collection until she could approach it with fresh enthusiasm and creativity. During this time she took on two new challenges: books on meditation directed specifically to teenagers and adults, published respectively as *InnerSpace* and *The Power of the Inner Self*. When she was ready, Maureen produced the new children's visualizations with renewed vitality, as you will discover in *Earthlight*.

Maureen had always intended *Earthlight* to be the completion of her cycle of children's meditations, although she had not anticipated that it would be the last of her books.

Maureen is survived by her beloved daughter Eleanor, to whom she dedicated each of her books, and who was the original inspiration for Maureen's innovative use of creative visualization with children.

Contents

Introduction

Welcome to *Earthlight,* the fourth of my collections of creative visualizations for children. In this introduction I explain the importance of meditation for children, both for their peacefulness, creativity, and growth during their early years, and for laying the foundations for an adult life of serenity and wellbeing. I also provide practical guidance on the use of the meditations.

Readers of my other books for children will already be familiar with some of what follows, which is of necessity repeated from the introductions of the previous books for readers new to my approach to meditation.

Earthlight completes my series of meditation books for younger readers, and joins *Starbright, Moonbeam,* and *Sunshine* in bringing the stars, the moon, the sun, and now the earth into the lives of children through the use of meditation.

Children and Their Growth

From the time of their birth, our babies live in complete trust, utterly dependent on us to care for them. We bathe them, feed them, play with them, and handle them lovingly in so many ways, ensuring they feel nurtured and loved. We clean their tiny bodies, finding it easy to kiss and cuddle these small parcels of delight. There is nothing we would not do to assist them to develop all their abilities. Perhaps you have experienced feelings of amazement that this small person is so totally in your care, if only for a short time.

Sometimes we can feel that our children will remain babies for a long time, but this is not so. Even though they will be dependent upon us for many years, they start to exert their independence in many ways early in life. Indeed, the personality of a child may be so different from those of his or her parents that they may even wonder how their child came to be born to them!

Each tiny person is amazingly complete and this becomes more obvious as time goes by. We notice how the hands and feet coordinate, and the body grows stronger. Each day is a revelation, and each year another milestone bringing so many changes. Babies are so receptive and cooperative, and the changes in the early part of a child's life are amazing. They learn to roll over, to sit up, to walk, to talk, and to run. Their body movements change as coordination develops in their bodies. Their speech patterns mature. They pay attention to what you and others say and do, and become adept at imitation. Sometimes their efforts appear to be a parody of who we are, and this can even make us take stock of what we say and do.

Children bring a completeness into our lives that we have not experienced before, as well as a kind of bonding different from anything we have previously encountered. Holding this small parcel of delight makes us both wonder at the immensity of the world that he or she is entering, and realize that they will be so totally in our care for only a short period of time. When our babies first come to us, it seems as though the years before they will leave us stretch far into the future, but as we watch them grow, as we go through each milestone with them, the time becomes shorter and shorter, until it is time for them to make their own way in life, as we ourselves have.

In fact, children become independent at an early age. The skill of crawling gives them a certain degree of independence, and walking still more. When they can manage to feed themselves without help, they have gone to yet another stage of their development of independence. These are just the forerunners of developing their strengths and their will to do things unaided becomes stronger.

Pre-school or infants' school allows children to become still further independent from the parental bonds. Their teachers become other role models of great influence, which takes them further in their quest for independence. Each step through primary and then secondary school furthers the process, until what was once a tiny bundle of dependence has moved to a far greater independence than we would have ever contemplated when we first beheld them as infants.

Through all this, most of us ensure our children receive the best schooling that we can afford. We encourage each stage of their mental and physical growth. We help them with their school work and listen to their problems. We help them deal with the emotional maze that friendships can be, as well as the disappointments that life can bring.

Life can be a difficult process for the young. When we look back on our own life and the mixed feelings we had about various issues we had to confront at an early age, we can understand how our own children may be perplexed by the attitudes or actions of their peers or others they have dealings with.

Children need to feel secure. While they are young, the family unit represents security. Having their own room, whether shared or not, with their own toys or animals around also helps their sense of security, as does going to school and having continuity of friends and teachers.

But there is a different sort of security that each of us needs, which is crucial for our development into an independent, confident person. It is not a security that comes from having particular things or people around. Ultimately, security is not about owning possessions or being dependent upon someone else. No person or thing can make us feel secure. Security is feeling good about one's self and so being secure within. This is achieved by each of us knowing ourself and this deep sense of security can be gained through meditation.

Meditation and Children

Meditation may seem like a heavy word when we speak of children or young people, or even of ourselves, but it is not. On the contrary, there is a lightness to it. Meditation does not restrict the mind. Meditation allows the mind to wander, to be at peace, to be free. It allows us to go deep within ourselves, to a quiet place where there is peace and tranquility. Meditation can help us to look at ourselves and our problems in new ways, and assist us in finding answers to our problems or to what we need in order to be happy.

Children have very receptive minds. From the time they are born, they are taking in information from their parents and other adults, their peers, and the environment. They are like a computer program, but one that grows and improves with age. They work with a simple program at first, then develop increasingly more complex ones as they mature.

Not only have they learned at an early age to feed themselves, crawl, and walk, they have learned complex communication skills by putting words and phrases together, often accompanied with hand actions. We do not know for sure when they start to put such things together, but

I feel they are assessing information from the time they are born. Most parents talk or sing to their children from the time of their birth, and I feel certain that the attention such children get, and the feelings that accompany the talking or singing, helps them in their development.

Whatever we feed into a child makes the adult. If we feed only positive, loving information into our children, we should then have their positive, loving thoughts going out into the universe as they mature and in turn have their own children; then the same process should be repeated with their own children. If we do not nurture children with love and kindness, then they may never know how to love others, let alone themselves or their own children.

Because we want the very best for our children, because we want to prepare them for the world they are to enter, we need to ensure that we care not only for their mind and body, but also for their spirit.

Meditation can help your child to nourish their body, their mind, and their spirit. Meditation has the means to allow us to go deep within the self. It allows us to constantly feed positive feelings and information to these three essential dimensions of the self.

Meditation and children go beautifully together. Children are receptive. Their minds are clear and clean like large pools of water, and they accept things readily and with ease. They do not query things as we do. If children are taught at an early age to meditate, they will find they will be able to meditate throughout their life, if they wish.

There are many different types of meditation, but I feel children relate best to the use of creative visualization in meditation. It enables their minds to be active, to draw pictures or images within, and for their creativity to flow. Children are invariably creative at something, whether it be drawing, coloring, constructing from building blocks, dancing, or putting words together to form stories. I believe we should encourage all forms of creativity in children while they are young, whether they end up being an artist, a dancer, a writer, or go on to be crane drivers, accountants, secretaries, join the armed forces, or become a world leader.

By teaching your child to meditate, you are teaching them that security lies within. If you teach them to meditate at an early age, you are preparing them for life and giving them an added advantage. If all children were taught to meditate and then went on to teach their children, the world would be a different place. People would be secure and happy within and unwilling to cause pain to others. I think that if we can encourage our children to meditate, not only will they be happier within themselves during their growing years, but they will end up being well-adjusted and contented adults.

Why I Started Meditation with my Daughter

In my first book, *Starbright*, I placed a lot of importance on the need for starting meditation with children as early as possible. I described how I started with my daughter, Eleanor, by doing simple visual exercises to quieten her at night when she was three years of age. Although she slept well, she had the occasional nightmare.

A nightmare is a terrible experience, both for the child and the parent. The child shakes and trembles while the parent wonders what has caused the distress. Is it something he or she has done? What is the child seeing in the waking hours to cause such troubled nights? Is it something in the bedroom that looks frightening in the darkened room?

Because of my concern, I gave Eleanor a Guardian Angel to make her feel safe. I explained how the wings of the Angel would go around her so she would feel protected and secure. I then placed Eleanor in a garden and drew a mental picture for her of what could be in her garden: perhaps lots of animals, perhaps a boat she could climb into, or a cloud to float on.

These exercises grew and grew as time passed until a key visualization emerged that I call "The Star Prelude." I gave Eleanor a Star and I brought its light down through her body; her Guardian Angel was there; I filled her heart with love; I gave her a Worry Tree where she could place anything that concerned her. Then I would give her a gate that, when opened, took her into her beautiful, secure, and serene garden.

Eleanor loved these times so much she wouldn't sleep until I had told her the meditation for the night. It became more than just telling her a story or visualization. We achieved a more complete way of bonding than I had experienced before, and a very beautiful one.

The meditations also tested my skills as a storyteller. I had never considered myself to be imaginative and never a teller of tales, yet, when I sat on the edge of Eleanor's bed, the images flowed. I always started with the Star, the light, the Angel, the heart, the Worry Tree, and the entrance to the garden. I would not have any idea what would follow nor what I would say. But when I opened the gate for Eleanor and we stepped into her garden, closing the gate quietly behind us, I always saw something that would give me the story for the night. Sometimes it would be just one thing, for instance, a cloud drifting by. Once I mentioned the cloud, other images would unfold, such as the cloud having reins and coming down to pick her up and take her off into the heavens. I was going into a state of meditation, too, so that the images I saw came from my subconscious and I was able to enjoy not only bringing them to Eleanor, but also experiencing them with her.

Eleanor still loves all the meditations that are included in *Starbright* and we have kept on using them, along with the meditations I have written in my later books for children, *Moonbeam* and *Sunshine*.

I still remember the first time I did the Panda Bear meditation (which appears in *Starbright*), and the look of sheer joy on Eleanor's face when I described the texture of the fur and how the Panda Bear would give her a big, big cuddle. We have used this meditation many times over the years, and there has always been the same reaction—joy and pleasure.

Eleanor loves being a fairy—she loves to fly—she loves to be with people—she loves her special garden. Eleanor was born in July 1981 and I think these meditations will stay with her for years to come. While I often think up new meditations for her, the old ones have become like evergreens—always wanted and loved.

In *Starbright* I included a number of meditations I had used with Eleanor and with many children who had stayed overnight. For many years these children would ask me to do a meditation for them when they stayed, even if they had not been with us for some time. And they always remembered the visualizations I had used before. I find it interesting that, in today's hustle and bustle, the children remember the quiet time they experienced during the meditation and wish to enjoy it again.

My small baby of yesteryear is now as tall as I am, becoming more and more independent, and more her own person. Eleanor is now sixteen years of age. I wrote *InnerSpace* when she went to secondary school, as I realized how her needs were changing and that children in their teens needed meditations and visualizations to help them prepare for their home work, to pass exams, to deal with peer pressure, to have career choices, and to have abundance in their lives.

Eleanor knows how to meditate and can easily reach the meditative state whenever she wants. However, there are still times when I will go and sit on the edge of her bed because she is upset by the pressures of the day or a personal problem, and take her through into the meditative state to ensure she has a peaceful night's sleep and awakes feeling refreshed, renewed, and free of the trauma she may have been experiencing the night before.

Children's Problems

We do not know what worries children have because they do not always have the ability to tell us. They may be too young or they may find themselves at a loss to express their feelings, and therefore find it extremely difficult to speak of their concerns. Their behavior may change and we will be concerned as to the reason. The child may say they are OK, either because they do not want to talk about the problem, or do not know how to express it.

In "The Star Prelude", which is used before each meditation, there is a Worry Tree (see page 27) that has been extremely helpful to the children who use it. Before entering the garden and commencing their meditation, they place their concerns and fears on the Worry Tree. They can pin their worries on the tree, tie them onto the branches, place them around the trunk, or just wish them to the very top of the tree. It is this tree's function to have the worries placed on its many strong and sturdy branches, and it can and does accept any worries and cares that the child wants to place there.

There are some pre-schools that have built an actual Worry Tree in the corner of a room so that the children, when they first arrive, can place their concerns immediately upon its branches or around its base, and have a day without the fears or concerns they felt when they first arrived. I was very pleased when I first heard this, as it is teaching the children skills at a very early age that will carry them through life, better equipped to deal with the problems they will face.

I know of one child (whose parents thought he didn't have a care in the world) who became extremely upset at the thought of placing all his worries on the Worry Tree. He worried about the Worry Tree being able to take all of the worries he was carrying around. Do we really know what worries our children have?

One child lost a grandparent and then a close neighbor who had cared for him. His parents knew he was concerned and upset by these losses, and found it helped him to put these concerns on the Worry Tree. The child also started leading the meditations for his parents and told them what worries they had to put on the tree! The family had been going through a difficult time with a failing business and a consequent move of house, plus numerous other causes of personal grief. Taking his parents through the meditation process and telling them what worries to place on the tree gave the child a feeling of control over the conditions that surrounded him. He placed the people who had passed over onto the Worry Tree and then said that his mother, father, and himself did not belong there. He then proceeded to take the entire family up and away into a world far removed from ours, where his mother (who in this life has short hair and often wears pants) had long flowing hair plus a long dress that floated freely through the air!

Another child had lost a family member and she constantly wanted her mother to read "Easter Morning," the traditional Easter meditation in *Starbright*. It says that there is no death, and that the spirit lives on. Not surprisingly, it was the child's favorite meditation because she needed that reassurance. The Worry Tree also assisted her during her grieving process.

Comments from Children

I met Sophia's mother at a book signing in December 1995. Sophia was five years old, a lovely sensitive Piscean who had no difficulty in seeing what her mother was describing to her. In fact, she experienced the visualization so clearly, that everything in the meditation felt extremely real to her. Sophia became very upset. She couldn't understand why what she saw in her meditation wasn't there when she opened her eyes. She cried and cried because she wanted what she experienced in her meditation to happen also in real life, for example, riding animals, traveling to the sun, going into the pool of reflection, playing with whales and dolphins, being a fairy, or whatever she had visualized in her meditative state. She found it difficult to understand that everything she saw so clearly in her meditation would not be happening in her outside world—and she wanted so much for it to be real.

Sophia's ability to perceive and feel everything so clearly is beautiful. It took a little while before she could accept that what she experienced was within herself and would not be repeated in her outer world. When she did accept this, her mother found that Sophia's creativity flowed and she could, for instance, change her stars each night, describing them in exquisite detail. What I found to be wonderful was that she not only had a Worry Tree but a Happy Tree, a Thankfulness Tree, and a Dream Tree. I wonder how many other trees she now has?

Rodney was twelve years old when I did a workshop for children with AIDS. He came from a different country and was a happy, lively boy with many questions to ask and an endless curiosity as to how things worked. When Rodney lived in his own country, he owned a duck and unfortunately a dog had eaten it. This episode was extremely distressing to him as he loved the duck deeply and the facilitators at the support group he attended said he often mentioned the duck and his loss. After doing the Star Prelude and a meditation from *Sunshine* called "The Traveling Armchair," Rodney did a drawing of what he saw and experienced. But he first drew the Worry Tree, and he placed his beloved duck at the base of the old tree's trunk. The Worry Tree did for him what it was supposed to do—it relieved his worries and gave him somewhere to place his duck where he knew it would be safe and secure.

Another child from the same AIDS Support Group, Rosemary, aged fourteen, drew the most beautiful garden imaginable, with the Grandfather

Tree inside the garden behind huge ornate gates (the Grandfather Tree is the oldest and wisest tree in the garden and is used in each of my books to the delight of the children). She sprinkled glitter upon the flowers so they would glow red and she included so much detail of the garden on her page that I was quite surprised. The opposite page was blank. She told me she had not had time to fill the page in, but would do so later. She said she was going to draw what she saw as her traveling armchair as it took her across the water to New Zealand where she visited a pine forest, and it was there that she scattered her father's ashes. Being able to travel in the meditative state and to scatter her dad's ashes was obviously something extremely important for her to do. I did not ask, but I assumed that she came from New Zealand and wanted him to rest there in peace. And what more peaceful place could you ask for than a pine forest?

How to Begin

The meditations in this book are, as in *Starbright*, *Moonbeam*, and *Sunshine*, only an indication of what you can do. There is no set format. You must feel comfortable with what you are doing and put the meditations into your own words, not mine. The ideas in the meditations may spark off scenes that you would like to explore with your child or children. Whatever I write is for guidance only and to suggest to your subconscious what you could say, not what you should say.

Each meditation begins with the Star (see page 25), the focal point for setting up the conditions for the meditation. Indeed, the Star is an integral part, the point where the relaxation and visualization starts. The Star is followed by bringing the white light down through the body, which is a wonderful relaxation exercise, and then the Angel—or you might prefer to say a wise person—that in turn can be followed by the Worry Tree (if you feel it is necessary).

You then do the meditation you have selected—perhaps "The Earth and Its Light," "The Time Machine," or "The Ant, the Grasshopper, and the Purple Bird." Select whichever you feel is appropriate to the mood of the child or children, or even to yourself.

Although I use a star as the focal point, you might prefer to use the moon or perhaps the sun. It does not matter which; the important thing is to give your child something to focus on. For relaxation and visualization, it is as easy to bring the light *down* from the sun or moon, as from a star.

If you use the moon, for instance, you could say that the moon's fingers are spreading out over the world so that everyone can see in the night, but there is one special moonbeam that is coming down just for your child. That moonbeam is filled with glitter, little sprinkles of which are touching all parts of their body, making it glow in the night.

And if it is the sun you have selected, you could speak about how the sun is a golden ball in the sky, filled with warmth and light. A large shaft of sunshine is dancing down to the child's bed where it is caressing and embracing them, filling every part of their body with the sun's rays. You must choose the vehicle with which you feel the most at ease, be it the sun, the moon, or the star.

How to Conclude

Each of the texts of the visualizations ends with an invitation for the child to continue in their meditation, taking off from any of the many suggestions made during the reading.

You may like to say to the child words such as, "I am going to be quiet now and leave you for a while. Let your mind be free. You are very safe and I will bring you back shortly." Leave them in their meditation for approximately five or ten minutes, according to their attention span, then bring them back by describing them now leaving their special garden, gently closing the gate behind themselves. Take them past the Worry Tree (although they are not to reclaim their worries), wrap them up in an imaginary golden cloak, and tell them to open their eyes when they are ready.

After the meditation, you may like to ask the child if they would like to tell you what they experienced during their meditation.

The Tone of Voice

When you first look at the meditations, you might think that they are not very long. Please remember that when you are speaking, you need to do so in a very slow, relaxed voice, pausing to let the scene sink in, so that the child, whose eyes are closed and who is focusing inwardly, can easily visualize and feel the scene.

The way you use your voice is very important. You will find it best to drop your voice by a few tones, speaking more and more slowly, with a soothing quality. There is something hypnotic about a voice that is low and relaxed.

Some of the meditations are a little longer than others. If you are tired, select a short one. I have found that children are not concerned with the length, only with the fact that *you* are doing it for *them*.

Although I call them meditations, you might prefer to call them stories or visualizations. This really is not important, it is only a name. The main thing is that you will be sharing a unique experience with your very special child.

Using the Mind

However, using these meditations with children is not the same as reading stories to them. Reading is passive in that the listener follows closely the author's story. Children do understand and become involved when we read a story, but in a guided meditation they become more actively involved. Reading a story and reading a meditation are different functions. Reading stories to children is a must because it introduces the child to the whole world of literature. It also helps the child to learn to read and spell. But meditation enables the mind to become free, to explore.

Each meditation has its own distinctive theme and gives children the opportunity to experience it. They make a film; they meet and can play music with the Ant, the Grasshopper and the Purple Bird; they travel to the sun in a sun vehicle; they enter a time machine; they can become a color; there is a magic car to take them wherever they want; they can enter the clock and change time. There are so many things they can do, and all these things bring their imagination to the fore. They can create these scenes in their minds and feel the sensations they bring. In other words, they participate in the meditation.

For Teachers

I taught meditation at my daughter Eleanor's infants' school, which proved to be an interesting experience for several reasons. Very few schools at that particular time, to my knowledge, encouraged meditation. Eleanor's teacher, Helen, who was also the head mistress, said she would like me to introduce meditation on a trial basis. So it was a first for me, a first for the children, and a first for the school.

The children were excited when they were asked to sit in a circle in order to meditate. I explained that we were trying something new and that meditation was like storytelling, only they would have their eyes closed while I drew a story or a series of pictures in their minds.

I read "The Star Prelude" and then one of my stories. From the time I started, we noticed that some children immediately went into a relaxed state and stayed motionless for the duration of the meditation. Others fidgeted; they could not sit still and had trouble keeping their eyes closed.

The children who went deeply into meditation, and stayed, happened to be the better students. The ones who fidgeted were children whose attention span was limited and who had difficulty concentrating in the normal course of learning.

Over the next few weeks, I spent time talking with the ones who could not settle. They were not sure what they were supposed to see nor what was expected of them. I explained that they might be able to see, in their imagination, what I was talking about and, if they could not, they might see something else they may wish to tell me about.

What surprised both Helen and me was that the children who were having the most difficulty with their studies were improving. They were able to think processes through, which was not possible before. The quality of their stories improved and showed a far better use of imagination.

At that time, I also helped the children "publish" their stories. They dictated them from their handwritten books and I typed them. Prior to learning meditation, their stories had been about their families, picnics, bikes, and so on, showing little use of their imagination, except for the few who naturally visualized well. Again Helen and I were surprised to find that the content of their stories changed and became more colorful, more imaginative, more creative.

Anything that can free a child's mind should be used. We end up being bound by various restrictions, which we must accept to get through life, but our minds should be free and active. Problem-solving becomes easier if the mind can see around corners instead of existing in the limited space to which many of us condemn it.

In the classroom, conclude the meditation as described in the earlier section, "How to Conclude."

After the meditation, ask each child what they saw or did. You will be surprised at what they say. Some see other worlds, some play with animals, some look, for instance, for the pot of gold at the end of the Rainbow meditation (which is in *Starbright)*. One girl said she saw "space" and described it beautifully. Her classmate, who was very much into space travel, snorted and said, "Don't be silly, you can't go into space without your space suit and helmet!"

Some children have a lot to relate; others are a bit shy of saying anything. If they were meditating for a short time at the start of each day rather than once a week, it would free them up immensely. I understand that if meditation is used prior to study, their efforts will be more fruitful.

I would like to emphasise again that the Worry Tree is very important. Children have many concerns we are not aware of. There could be sibling rivalry, difficulties in the home, or problems with school friends. How often have our children heard the phrase, "I'm not going to be your friend any more," and how often have we had to dry the resultant tears?

Meditation for All

Meditation is a time for reflection and contemplation, a time to go within. It is not beyond the reach of anyone, provided they take the time and create the opportunity.

Meditation is very simple: you need to sit quietly either on your own or with a group of people. (It is best to sit in an upright chair—if you make the chair too comfortable, you may fall asleep.) Wear loose clothing for comfort but, if that is not possible, loosen anything that is tight around your waist or neck so that you do not feel these restrictions. Try not to cross your arms and legs as this can lead to discomfort.

You may like to have soothing music in the background or prefer silence. Sometimes I like to fix a scene in my head, such as the garden in which I place the children. At other times my mind is like a blank screen ready to receive whatever images happen to cross it.

The brain works at different levels of consciousness. These levels are called Beta, Alpha, Theta, and Delta. Beta is our normal conscious level, the level at which we work in our daily lives. When we go into a meditative state we are going into Alpha, which enables us to create scenes and images on the screen of our mind. There are also the Theta and Delta levels, which we can attain as we go more deeply into the meditative state. Most of us work very well simply within the Alpha level, coming back to our normal conscious state feeling refreshed and renewed.

It is up to the individual to decide how long to spend in meditation. If you can only spare five or ten minutes that can be ample. However, twenty minutes is better if you wish to feel the full benefit; meditation can promote calmness, relax tension, and give relief from anxiety as you become detached from your problems. Your problems will not necessarily go away, but meditation can help you in handling problems. And sometimes the solution to a problem comes when we take the time to sit quietly.

Meditation is a very soothing, relaxing way of coping with the stresses and anxieties of daily life. Many doctors recommend meditation as a wise and good practise for their patients. It is a relaxing and pleasant way to spend a short period of time, and one that has many benefits.

Why not teach these skills to our beloved children as early as possible? And why not demonstrate to them the benefits of meditation by practicing it ourselves?

Tomorrow's Adults

The children of today are the adults of the future. We need to ensure they have the necessary tools to cope with what life is going to present to them. If you think back on your own childhood, coming into your teens, and facing the future with great excitement as well as trepidation, then you know that this is also how your children will feel. If we had been taught at their age to have a solitary space within ourselves where we can be still and at peace, I am sure we would have faced our future with a far more confident sense of ourselves.

By teaching the children of today how to meditate, how to feel a sense of peace and security within that no one can take from them, we are preparing them for the tomorrows where they will face many high points, and also many low points.

Give your child or children the tools to equip them for every eventuality by teaching them meditation, by finding their own inner space that will help to give them a security of self that money and society cannot—and they in turn will pass on to their own children what you have taught them. Then our world will be a better, more positive place where there is hope for all.

The Star Prelude

I WANT you to see above your head a beautiful, beautiful Star. This Star is very special to you, as it is your very own Star. It can be any color you like—you might see it as being a purple star, or perhaps a pink one—or blue—or yellow—or is it a speckled star? Or a silver one? Because it is your very own Star, it can be any color or colors you choose.

This special Star is filled with white light, lovely white light which shimmers and glows. I want you to see this light streaming down toward you until it reaches the very top of your head. And now I want you to bring this pure light down through your head and take it right down your body until your whole body is filled with this glorious white light.

I want you to feel the light going down your arms, right down, until you feel it reaching your hands and going into each and every finger.

Feel that light going down the trunk of your body, down until it reaches your legs, and when you feel it there, take it right down until it comes to your feet and then feel the light going through each toe.

I now want you to look into your heart and to fill your heart with love for all the people and animals in the world. They are your friends, be they large or small. Can you see your heart getting bigger and bigger? It's expanding because you have so much love in your heart for all these people and the animals, and of course for yourself.

Now your Guardian Angel is waiting to wrap golden wings of protection around you before taking you into your garden. The Angel's wings are very large and very soft, just like down. Everyone has their own Guardian Angel and that Guardian Angel takes care of you and protects you always, so you are never alone. It's important to remember this and to know that you have someone who looks after you with love and care.

Your Guardian Angel is now going to take you to a garden that is your own special place, but before you enter I want you to look at the large tree that is outside. This tree is called the Worry Tree. I want you to pin on this tree anything that might worry you—perhaps you have had some arguments at school, or maybe you are having difficulty with your school work. This tree will take any worries at all, be they with your friends or your family. This tree accepts anything that you would like to pin there.

Your Guardian Angel is now opening the gate for you to enter, and as you go in you find the colors are like nothing you have seen before. The beauty of the flowers, the colors, the textures, and the perfume—breathe them in. The grass is a vivid green and the sky a beautiful blue with little white fluffy clouds. It is very peaceful in your garden; it is full of love and harmony.

You may feel this prelude is very long, but it is wise to create with care, thought and feeling the scene your child is entering. When your child is used to it, the prelude may be shortened, as it is not always necessary to describe the Star and the Angel in such full detail. Then the prelude will become something like the shorter version that follows.

I want you to see above your head a beautiful, beautiful Star. This Star is filled with lovely white light. I want you to bring the white light from that Star right down through your body until you can feel it in every part of your body, and your heart is filled with love for all humanity and for all creatures, great and small.

Your Guardian Angel is waiting for you to wrap a golden cloak of protection around you and take you to the Worry Tree. Put anything that worries you on the tree, and then your Guardian Angel will open the gate and take you inside your garden.

Your garden is filled with glorious flowers; the grass and the trees are an emerald green, and the sky a deep blue with little white clouds.

After you have set the scene, as it were, you can do anything with the children that you think they would enjoy. Become a child again yourself—I think you will be surprised at what pleasure these flights of fantasy will give you.

The meditations that follow in this book and those in three of my other collections—*Starbright*, *Moonbeam*, and *Sunshine* — have been used with children of all ages. I have incorporated different themes that I feel will appeal to both the adult and the child. Indeed, you may like to use some of these meditations for yourself, along with those in my collections written specifically for adults and teenagers, *The Inner Garden* and *InnerSpace*.

I have found that many adults buy and use my "children's" books for themselves, even some who have no children nor plan to have them. We all retain a child within us, one who needs to be fed, nurtured, and cared for.

The Golden Lion

YOU CAN feel the warmth of the sun caressing your face and body as you enter your garden, and the earth feels warm beneath your feet. Your pathway winds in and out of the many tall trees that stand as sentinels of protection, and small animals scurry among the undergrowth. Some of them pause and peek out at you because they are sometimes a little shy.

The flowers stand tall and serene, their brilliant colors

mingle together and their perfume drifts toward you as you go deeper within your garden. There are many birds circling overhead and they seem to be making for the clearing where the Grandfather Tree lives. Perhaps you would like to make your way there to see what is happening.

You hear quite a lot of chattering going on when you reach the Grandfather Tree. The parrots in all their beautiful colors have landed on his branches and are talking to one another with their loud voices, while the other birds speak in a quieter way. The branches of the Grandfather Tree are beckoning you to come closer. As you do so, you notice small rabbits sitting around his trunk and that there is a sleepy lion lying nearby. He is stretching his paws toward the sun's light, twitching his body slightly as he enjoys the warmth on his fur and limbs.

Why don't you go closer to the lion and stroke his fur, so that you can feel the warmth of the sun on his body entering your hand? This magnificent lion flicks his tail slowly as he enjoys the movements you are making on his body, and he rolls over onto his back so that you can stroke his stomach. He loves having his stomach scratched and he lets out small sounds of delight as you do so.

This magnificent tawny-colored lion has a huge mane of fur surrounding his head and the gentle breeze lifts it, moving it this way and that. Why don't you pat his mane, moving his fur in all directions? As you do so, he stretches his body with pleasure at having you so close to him, and especially at feeling your fingers moving through his mane.

Look at the pads on the lion's feet and you will see how thick they are from walking across all sorts of terrain, some soft and some hard.

This lion has many stories to tell. Why don't you curl up near him and listen to them? The Grandfather Tree is shading you so that the sun's light is filtering through his branches, and the many birds in their powerful bold colors are becoming quieter as they too want to listen to this old lion and his tales of adventure.

As you listen to him, you feel as though you too are experiencing what he went through. His mother and father used to go hunting when he was a tiny cub, leaving him with his brothers and sisters to play. They played by charging at rocks, and by trying to climb them, even ones that were too big for them. They also loved to chase butterflies, which would fly in all directions, their beautifully colored wings shining in the sun's light as they dipped and soared toward the blue of the sky.

The lion and his brothers and sisters used to meet other small animals and play with them too, and they enjoyed all the games they invented. Your golden lion is telling you how their hearing became so acute that they could hear their parents returning from way, way off, and how he and his brothers and sisters would bound down the slopes to meet them.

This lion with his beautiful tawny coat has many adventures to tell. As he grew older, he traveled to many places where he saw and experienced many, many things. He will always be happy for you to return to him at any time, so that he can tell you more of his stories.

He stands up now, shaking his large mane, and lets loose a huge roar as though to awaken the whole of your special garden and all those who live there, and to let them know he is about to move on yet again. Why don't you put your hand upon his mane and accompany him on one of his journeys? Who can tell where you will end up …

The Camera and the Photographs

THERE ARE many daffodils and primroses blooming in your garden, and their perfume drifts through the bushes and trees, touching their leaves gently. The sky is a deep indigo blue and huge, ballooning white clouds float by. The golden sun is sending its warmth down.

There is a pathway before you that is winding in and out of the trees. I want you to walk down that path until you come to the Grandfather Tree, the oldest tree in your garden. There are many colored birds sitting on his branches, preening their feathers and making soft cooing noises.

You see that there is a small seat with a red padded cushion near the Grandfather Tree's thick trunk. Why don't you sit on this comfortable seat and look around? You may notice some small rabbits peeping out from beneath the nearby bushes, and perhaps some of the birds may leave the Grandfather Tree's branches to sit upon your shoulders.

If you look around carefully, you will see something nestled underneath the branches of the Grandfather Tree. Why, it's a camera. The Grandfather Tree has been taking care of this camera and has been waiting for you to collect it. Now one of his branches is holding it out to you and his leaves rustle as he speaks. Can you hear what he is saying to you?

I think he would like you to take this camera and photograph the many birds that are sitting on his branches. Or perhaps you could place the camera on a stand, put its timer on slow, and take a photograph of yourself with the birds upon your shoulders. After that, you could take photographs of the clouds above, which have begun to form faces. Or perhaps you would like to capture the light coming through the trees, or even try to photograph the rabbits, who can be a little shy.

The Grandfather Tree is now saying that this special camera can take photographs for you of your past, your present, and your future. You already know your past and you are in your present. I wonder what your future will be?

If you choose to look at your future, why don't you fix into your mind what you want? Then press the button on the camera and, zoom, there it is! If you place the photograph in front of you, you can enter the picture and experience what your future will be like. You might see yourself leaving school and going to live in another place, or perhaps you may see yourself being a lion tamer, or traveling into space.

Going into the future can be very exciting, as there are so many different things that you can do. You may think of something else you would like to do, so fix your mind on it, take another photograph and go into it.

Going back to your past would be fun too. You may decide to go back to when you were a little baby, or a very small child just starting to walk. Take a photograph of when you were learning how to walk. Can you imagine what it was like learning something that you do so easily in your present life?

Then again, maybe you would like to take lots of photographs of the present and put them all into a book that you can treasure forever. These photographs of the present will becomes memories of your past for you to look back on.

You could even include some photographs of the different futures you have gone forward to. I wonder what you will do …

The Earth and Its Lights

IT IS very quiet and peaceful in your garden. Feel the freshness of the air and the serenity that surrounds you. The animals are coming forward to greet you, as they always do. You may see an animal from your past, perhaps a favorite dog, cat, or bird; maybe even a parrot or a mouse—or you might choose an animal to accompany you that would normally not come close. All the animals coexist peacefully in your garden and they like being called forward when people enter their special place.

The blue of the sky is enriched by the green of the slender trees thrusting their branches and leaves high into the air. The birds dart to and fro, picking up little twigs to build nests to settle into, within the comfort and security of the trees' branches.

There are many lights that come to earth from many different places. There is the starlight, the moonlight, and the sunlight. All of these lights come to earth to enrich our lives, to make us feel warm, to make us feel happy, to make us feel bright, to make us feel special.

The sun's light makes us feel warm and protected and it encourages growth on our earth. The trees and flowers flourish from being nurtured by its light.

The light from the moon bathes our world in light and shadow, making a beautiful play as its light dapples through the trees and lands on our homes. The moon is full of mysteries that many people would like to solve. Would you believe that some people think the moon is made of green cheese? Or that some people think they can see someone living on the moon who looks as though he is a very old man? I wonder if an old person really does live there? And I wonder who lives on the far side of the moon, which we cannot see?

All of these lights come to the earth to bathe us with their energy. They make us feel good about ourselves and about being alive.

Why don't you allow these fingers of light to come around you and play with you?

First, stretch out your arms to the sky and try to catch a sunbeam as it touches our body. The sun's fingers dart away from you and then return, playing hide and seek with you through the foliage of the trees.

Now the sun sets, but rather than focusing on it disappearing below the horizon, you could look carefully for the first stars to appear in the darkening sky. You notice that the stars twinkle as though they have a sense of humor and are playing a game of "See if you can see me."

Now the moon's gentle glow surrounds you, making you feel as light as a fairy or an elf. If you look around your special garden in the moon's light, you may see the fairies and elves coming out to play. The little people like to dance and sing when the stars and the moon shine down. And during the daytime they are busy flying to and fro within the sun's light.

Why don't you wander around your garden, feeling these different lights and energies, and playing with the elves and the fairies? Perhaps you would like to sing and dance too …

Being a Color

YOU CAN feel the warmth of the sun's rays caressing your body as the light breeze moves through your hair. The sun's light is shining through the trees and settling around the flowers, encouraging their growth. The flowers are sending out their beautiful perfumes into the fresh air, to mingle with the smell of the rich earth.

There are so many colors in your garden. There isn't just one shade of green but many different variations. Some greens are light, some dark, and some have a yellowish tinge. Even the red roses vary in color and shade. Some reds are deep and strong, and others are bright and glowing.

Have you ever thought about becoming a color? I think it would be fun. You could change from one to another, or even be all the colors of the rainbow, unless you prefer to stay the one color.

You could be red for a while and have all the energy that red brings with it. Red makes you want to do things and be noticed. It makes you feel vibrant and alive, and it enables you to stand out.

Yellow makes you feel bright and glowing. There are yellow daisies and huge golden sunflowers standing tall, reaching for the sun. Yellow excites your mind, so that you always want to know how things work.

What about gold? To become a golden color would be like becoming a brightness that shines and glows, like the golden sun that hangs in the sky. Gold is a rich color that brings happiness and life with it.

The beautiful blue of the sky will make you feel gentle. There are blue bells and blue birds, and, of course, the sea reflects the sky's blue. If you would like to feel the blue of the sea, you could become the blue water, with little white tops on your waves.

Each color can make you feel differently. Purple is rich and deep and can make you feel dreamy and very special, while violet can bring out your creativity.

Perhaps you may like to think about being silver? It must be nice to be so bright and shiny. Water looks like silver when it falls, as the sun's light catches and transforms it.

There are so many colors that you can become. You can be green like the trees, brown like the earth, or blue like the sky and water. You can be any color you like.

In fact, if you decide to become brown like the earth,

you might even start to feel what the earth is like. You may feel the firmness that the brown earth has in some places, and then this feeling may change from those earthy textures to the golden sands of the beaches or deserts. Then you will be able to experience how the sand feels as it shifts beneath people's feet.

Green feels lovely and fresh and you may feel yourself growing with the green as the trees do. You may even feel the trees' roots growing deep within the earth, taking the water as nourishment for their roots so that the leaves grow greener and greener, shining with health.

There are so many things you can do with colors. You could be yellow like a canary and perhaps feel what it would be like to sing like one.

Why don't you mix your colors up? Be red for a while, and then change to orange, then yellow, green, blue, white, mauve, violet, purple—or whatever colors you wish . . .

The Steamboat

SO MANY wonderful things happen when you are in your special garden. The air is always clean and the perfume from the flowers drifts around you. The trees bend their heads and nod to you, waving their branches excitedly as you walk by. They seem to be telling you something. If you listen carefully, you can hear what they are saying.

They are telling you to go further along the pathway as there is a surprise waiting for you. You hear a sound like steam escaping and a whistle blowing. I wonder what that can be? If you keep walking you will come to a large river where there is a very large and graceful steamboat. The paddles move through the water, turning around and around, and their motion gently rocks several small boats drifting nearby.

The steamboat is white with black trim and the funnel has a green band going around it. I wonder what the name of this boat is? I feel it hasn't been given a name as yet. Perhaps you could think of one and paint it on the side of the boat. I wonder what you will call it?

The inside of the steamboat is made of brown polished wood and the floor shines beneath your feet. The motion of the boat takes a little getting used to as it ploughs through the water, throwing up a silver spray on either side. At first you may find it difficult to get your sea legs, but it won't take long before you feel as though walking while the boat is moving is as normal as walking on the earth.

The navigation instruments are bright and shiny, and the ship's wheel is large and has gold trim. Someone must look after them very well because they look as though they are polished every day. If you ask the captain, I am sure you will be allowed to steer the boat down the river. He will show you how to navigate and to steer a straight course, so that you do not run into other boats on the water.

There are musicians playing on the boat and their lively music drifts across the water. All those on board the other boats that bob on the water enjoy the music coming from the steamboat.

The river has many green trees and bushes that overhang its sides, and the weeping willow trees shade many smaller plants, their graceful fingers trailing through the water.

The captain is going to leave you in charge while he goes below to rest. He is handing you his captain's hat to wear. It has gold braid on it and the brim peaks over your forehead.

There is a large golden bell near the wheel. Why don't you ring it so that the other craft on the water will hear the sound and know that you are nearby?

Keep navigating and steering the boat down the wide river that curves in front of you. I wonder where the river will take you …

The Walking Boots

VERY TINY puffs of clouds are scudding across the beautiful blue sky. The sun hangs high above you, like a giant golden ball in the sky, spreading its light out to all who care to feel it.

The large trees in your garden are bending and moving their branches as they feel the breeze gently ruffling their leaves. They are shaking themselves ever so slightly. The birds that have made their homes there fly off, high into the sky.

Look around you. There are many deer coming through

the trees and rabbits are emerging from their burrows. They love to feel the sun on their fur.

The Grandfather Tree is shaking his branches in welcome, and his leaves seem to be shielding something from your view.

If you part his leaves, you will find a pair of boots sitting there. They are made of the finest brown leather and their laces are brightly colored, with the colors red, gold, and green woven into one strand.

Why don't you try these special boots on? They seem to be the right size for you and they feel so comfortable that you want to walk and go exploring in them. These boots are perfect for walking. With them you can walk for as long as you wish, and yet you will never feel tired.

As you walk, if you stretch your feet a little inside the boots, you will notice that you can take longer and longer strides.

And if you press down on the soles, you can take gigantic leaps that can take you from one place to another. Now this is fun! Press down and see if you can leap and touch the top of that tree in front of you. Perhaps you could even leap over the tree and land on the other side. The Grandfather Tree is shaking with laughter as you do this.

You can do so many things with these boots. Try experimenting with the length of your stride as you walk through your garden. You could take tiny steps and then large ones, and then leap through the air.

These wonderful boots can take you the longest distance in the shortest time. Why, I imagine you could be in China in next to no time, or perhaps India or Africa. Or maybe there is some other special place you would like to go to.

Why don't you practice doing leap frogs over the trees before deciding where you want to go …

The Vegetable Kingdom

GO FORWARD along the path that is before you, feeling, as always, the peace and quiet and serenity that exists here. Smell the freshness of the flowers. Perhaps you could pick one, placing it into one of your button holes or behind your ear. Watch where you have taken the flower from and you will see another flower forming to take its place. In your special garden nothing ever dies.

There, in front of you, is the vegetable kingdom. All the

vegetables seem very large and you may feel very small as you wander around them.

That large white vegetable is a cauliflower, with protective green leaves surrounding it. It has some water dripping from its leaves and, if you shake them, the drops will fall around you like a shower.

And what is that? Why, it must be the largest zucchini you have ever seen. Its skin is bright green and shiny and you can use it as a slippery dip if you wish. Climb up to the top and you will be able to slide all the way down to the bottom.

Is that rhubarb growing over there? Pull the leaves aside and you will find that there is a space within where you can hide. You can now peek out and not be seen. I wonder what you will see?

There are many vegetables and fruits growing here. Can you name them all? I can see trees with apples and oranges; there are strawberry and blackberry bushes; there are apricot trees, banana trees, and many plum trees. The plums are a rich red and their skin is soft to the touch.

Aren't those tomatoes large? You feel like climbing to the top of the reddest tomato and sliding down.

There are also potatoes and carrots, spinach and broccoli, peas and beans, and even sweet potato.

I wonder who looks after all these fruits and vegetables? If you look closely, I am sure you will see that there are small people who nurture and care for them. The banana people dress in yellow and the ones who look after the spinach and broccoli are in green. Because there are red and green apples, the clothing of their carers is in both colors.

Why don't you choose one of the vegetables or fruits to care for? If you do, the little people will give you clothing to put on that is the right color. You may even decide to change after a time and go to a different fruit or vegetable, and that is all right. If you do, your clothing will change to the appropriate color.

You can have fun hiding inside some of the unusual fruits and vegetables in your garden, and perhaps you could spray a little water onto the little people when they are not looking, which will make them laugh …

The Magic Car

FEEL THE freshness of the air on your rosy cheeks as you wander down your winding pathway. As you walk, smell the sweet scent from the lovely flowers that surround you.

Your garden is full of excitement, and even the trees seem to be moving more than usual. There are many birds in the sky and some of them have come to land on the Grandfather Tree. He is beckoning for you to come near his large trunk so that he can bend to whisper in your ear. Give him a big hug, and feel his energies flowing into your body, making you stronger and stronger. Lean against him while he whispers into your ear about a special present he has for you. And now look into the clearing in front of the old tree to see what it is.

Why, it is a magnificent car that is revving its motor in preparation for take-off. This beautiful car has been waiting for you to come into your garden and to sit behind its wheel.

It has many colors and someone must have spent a long time polishing it, because it is so very shiny. The body of this car has been painted a deep rich red. Its fat bumper bars are bright green and there is an emblem painted on the doors in gold. The steering wheel is covered in golden mesh and the dashboard is made of silver, with controls made from precious black stones.

Look, the driver's door is opening for you. Why don't you climb in and slide behind the wheel? The car begins to play your favorite music as it closes its door behind you.

There are many instruments in front of you, all winking

and blinking. Now that the car's door has closed, all you have to do is to hold onto the wheel, and tell the car where you want to go. You can allow the car to drive itself for you or, if you like, you can steer the car yourself moving from left to right, then straightening it up after going around corners. Or you can simply let the car do all the driving for you.

Some of the birds have decided to join you on your journey and they fly in formation around you as you take off. Your magic car is going round and round in the clearing, getting you used to the driving. The Grandfather Tree is shaking his branches and saying he will be there when you return.

Now try slowly pulling on the steering wheel as you tell the car, "lift off." It is now gently taking off from where you have been, rising high above the treetops. Now push down on the wheel and your car will dip down, giving you a different view of your garden.

Isn't it fun? I wonder where you can go? Perhaps to the

other side of the world, or perhaps to visit your friends. Or maybe you will skim up over the treetops, then high above the world to the moon or another planet. This magical car can take you wherever you want to go. I wonder where you will choose to go …

The Film

THE TREES are waving their arms in welcome as you enter your garden, and they are showing you the way to a clearing. Many animals have come to this clearing and are sitting, waiting for you. The flowers are sending out their different perfumes and they blend into a lovely fragrance that the gentle wind takes into the air. The Grandfather Tree is proudly preening his branches and moving them around in the air, sending birds scattering as he gently shakes himself. The birds return as he settles down, gathering on his branches and waiting because they know something is going to happen.

Look around and you will notice that your garden is beginning to look like a film set. There are people putting props around and the cameras are being rolled into place to commence shooting a film. There is a green director's chair that has your name on the back and there is a megaphone next to it so that people will be able to hear when you give your orders.

What fun it would be to make a movie. You could sit in your chair, be the director, and make a movie. Why don't you make your own? I wonder what type of movie you would like to make? It could be a Western … or an action film … or perhaps one about traveling to other parts of the world … or outer space … or it could be about your friends … or your family.

Because the animals have come to be around you,

perhaps you would like to make a film about the animal kingdom. It could be about a particular breed of animal, or you may decide to do a documentary that includes many different species. You may like to do one about the animals you have at home, or the animals you wish were there. You could even make a comedy, if you like, and perhaps include animals that you are unlikely to have at home. Have you thought about sharing your house with a lion or a giraffe? If you chose to have a giraffe staying with your family, I think you would have to raise the roof because of its high neck. And wouldn't it be fun if the lion sat in your dad's favorite chair and refused to move when your dad wanted to sit there to watch TV or read his paper?

Perhaps you would like to film a family who laugh and share many good times together. Maybe they are celebrating their birthdays or opening Christmas presents underneath a huge tree. You could include some difficult times and show

how the family work together as one to make things better and to make everyone happier.

If you wanted, you could do a film about your school that would include your teachers and friends. It could record the different things you do and learn. Perhaps it could be entitled, "A Day in My Life at School." Your family would love to see what you do there. Or perhaps you could shoot a film of a day at the beach or at the zoo.

Because you are the director, you can place people, or animals for that matter, wherever you want on the set. Sit in the green director's chair that has your name on the back. There are many large cameras around with plenty of sound equipment and lighting.

Although there are any number of things you could do, just select one for now. I wonder which you will choose? When the cameras are ready to roll, don't forget to call out: "lights—camera—action" …

The Earth

YOUR GARDEN is peaceful and the sky a gentle blue with puffs of clouds drifting past. There are many strawberry and mulberry bushes with ripened fruit waiting to be picked. Perhaps you could put some into a small basket and take them with you as you wander down your pathway.

The earth feels warm underneath your feet and many small insects are busy on the pathway. The earth brings many things to us. It allows its surface to be used not only by us but also by the trees and other plants, by the seas, lakes, rivers and other waterways, and by deserts and rainforests. Of course, it is also used by the insects, the mammals, the fish, the birds, and all the other animals.

I wonder what it would be like to go inside the earth and to be at the center of the world? If you look carefully, you will notice that there is a door in the ground in front of you. If you pull the door up, you will find there is a winding staircase that will take you down deep into the earth's core.

The main passageway has lights on the walls so that you can see where you are going, and there are many other passageways leading off that are also well lit.

For the time being, stay in the main passageway as this will bring you to a landing that overlooks the earth's core. It feels warm on this landing, but not hot, and from here you can see people working to make this warmth come out from the center of the earth to where you normally live.

This whole inner area is filled with large machinery with many dials and knobs and flashing lights. If you look closely, you will find that most of the earth's conditions are pre-programmed and need very little alteration.

The inner-earth people ensure that the machinery is kept in good working order, so that the temperatures do not vary greatly from what people on the surface of the earth are used to, no matter where they live.

However, the inner-earth people can change the temperatures if they want to. If you ask, they will show you how to put warm earth in one part of the world, dry deserts into another, and ice into other regions.

One section of the machinery deals entirely with the seas, the lakes, and the rivers that are spread over so much of the land. And look, this lot of machinery deals with the trees and bushes, and another with the flowers.

I wonder what would happen if you changed one of

these dials to read, "Put water on the Sahara Desert?" Would flowers and trees then grow there?

There is so much you could do, being at the center of the earth. If you warmed the earth more in certain places, perhaps the people who lived there could experience what it would be like to live in a tropical climate instead of with snow. And then, if you lessened the warmth in other areas, those people would then be able to feel what it is like to live in cooler conditions, perhaps like the Antarctic.

I wonder what changes you will make …

The Statue

THE SKY in your garden is a beautiful sapphire blue and you feel the warmth of the golden sun moving through your body.

Your garden is peaceful, so quiet you can hear the ants moving around in the grass and on the trees. The air is crystal clear and you can feel a gentle breeze caressing your cheeks and touching your hair.

I want you to go further into your garden until you come to a clearing. This clearing is surrounded by large green trees, and in the center is a tall stone statue. I wonder what it is doing here? Why don't you go forward and look at it?

The statue is huge and towers high above you. Perhaps you could climb up until you can sit on the statue's arm. From there you have a good vantage point and can see a long way ahead, as well as around you below. If you stand on its arm, you will find that the statue is so tall that your head only reaches its neck.

Birds are coming to rest on the statue's head and butterflies of many colors are flying around the statue. I wonder what it is like to be a statue? If you could climb inside this statue maybe you will find out.

If you look carefully you will see a small door on the side of the statue's neck, which isn't very far for you to climb. As you go up, look at the face and you will notice that the eyes are very still and blank, as are the other features of its face.

Now that you are inside, you will see a small set of stairs

that take you up into the head. It is quite a long climb, but when you get there you can peek out from holes in the stone eyes and look at your surroundings, seeing them as the statue does.

I wonder what it would be like to bring this statue to life? And wouldn't people be surprised to see not only the statue moving, but that the eyes are colored and winking at them?

Why don't you turn yourself, for a short while, into the statue? You could then look out at the world and know you can't be seen. You now have birds nesting on your head, which is fun. They are talking to each other as they move about, their small claws holding them in place.

Why don't you move the statue's arms and legs and go for a walk? It may seem a bit jerky at first, but you will soon get the hang of it. I wonder where you will go? Why don't you go to a beach? It might be nice for the statue to look out onto different surroundings.

Or perhaps you could go to the mountains. Because the

statue is so tall it can take very long strides and so take you wherever you want to go in no time.

You could go to a number of different places and see where the statue feels the most comfortable. Or you could, after visiting various places, return to where you were. I will leave it up to you …

The Time Machine

FEEL THE freshness of the air against your skin and breathe it in, cleansing your lungs. The sun's rays fall around you, warming your body. Feel the warmth and peace that surrounds you in your garden, making you feel good.

The many colored butterflies are coming forward to greet you and are flying round your head and body. Some are settling gently on your shoulders and hair.

They are wanting to lead you to a special place where

you have not been before. Why don't you follow them? They are flying in front of you, except for the ones that have settled on your shoulders, their small wings tickling your face as they move their wings backward and forward.

They seem to be saying, as they settle on the bushes in front of you, to pull the bushes to one side so you can see what is hidden inside.

Look, there is a machine that appears to be very old, almost as though it has come through time. Perhaps it has, and it has landed in your very own garden.

Even though it appears old, it has a shiny surface and looks as though it has been lovingly cared for. Why don't you open the door and step inside?

The interior is much larger than you expected. The control panel looks as though it may be difficult to use and is surrounded by large columns with unusual writing on them. Why don't you sit at the controls and see if you can decipher the writing? I imagine it will tell you about time and where this machine will take you.

There is a small yellow button in front of you. If you push it, you will hear a voice telling you that this is a time machine, a machine that will take you back in time if that is where you want to go, or even forward into the future.

Why don't you go back in time? You could visit all sorts of countries at different points in their history. Let me see, where would you like to go? Perhaps back to Atlantis, which disappeared beneath the seas so many years ago, or you may want to go to the time of the ancient Egyptians, when they were building the pyramids. You could even go back to when cave men and women cooked wild animals over an open fire, which they lit by rubbing sticks together.

Or you could go forward into the future. You could look at the future of this world, or perhaps the future of another world.

There are so many different times and places you could

go to, and you have the time to choose whichever you wish. Remember that you can go backward or forward in time with this machine. The time machine will remain in your garden for you to enter and use whenever you wish …

The Big Top

YOU FEEL full of joy and happiness as you wander through your special garden. The air is fresh against your skin and you can feel something quite exciting is going to happen in your garden. There is a stillness in the air, a hushed feeling of expectancy as though the air itself is not sure of what will happen.

Keep walking down your garden path as you always do, stopping to talk to the trees and the animals on the way. The trees are whispering to each other as you pass close by. Can you hear what they are saying? And the four winds are whistling through the trees' branches as they come to visit. Listen carefully … Why, they are saying that near the Grandfather Tree is the Big Top where all sorts of exciting things happen.

Why don't you go to the Grandfather Tree and sit on one of his lower branches? From there you can watch as the people erect the tent. They are very busy driving the pegs into the ground and then pulling on the ropes to straighten the tent—and there it is, rising high into the sky. The tent is striped red, green, and yellow, and it has a large golden flag at the top that flickers in the breeze.

There is a man coming toward you and he is wearing a tall black hat, and his fitted suit is of shiny black material. His shirt is white with ruffles down the front, and he has high black boots and a long whip that he is cracking in the air.

He is know as the the Ringmaster or the Master of Ceremonies and he is now calling out your name.

You notice that the Ringmaster is carrying a suit similar to his own, on a hanger in his left hand, together with a small whip. This suit looks as though it is the right size for you. What fun it would be to be the Ringmaster. Why don't you put the clothes on—as I am sure they will fit—and go into the Big Top with him?

The smell of the sawdust is strong in the air and the animals are excited at the prospect of performing for you and the audience.

The music starts and the Ringmaster takes you to the center of the arena. He cracks his whip high in the air, and then waits for you to also send yours crackling through space. Don't worry; the whip is not used on the animals. It is only for show and to announce the arrival of the various acts.

As you announce each of the acts, you could make your

whip crack as it whistles through the air. You could perhaps start by bringing on the clowns, who always put people into a happy mood before the other acts.

And then perhaps it could be the dancing horses, who always place their hoofed feet so prettily as they move around the ring of the Big Top.

The lions are always impatient to come out and to roar and growl before they leap through their ring of fire. And everyone always gasps when the trapeze artists swing high in the Big Top, before flying through the air to their partner who catches them.

There are many acts lined up to come on. Some of the horses have monkeys swinging on their backs doing tricks and turning cartwheels, and the fire-eating people are practicing in the wings. I wonder who you would like to bring on next …

The Moonbeam Fairy and the Wishing Well

THE LIGHT from the moon streams around you, its fingers of light highlighting the pathway and making it very easy for you to walk along. It seems different to walk within your special garden at night, but you feel very safe and secure and comfortable as you do so. The moon's light is so inviting that you feel you have to investigate why the moon has drawn you to join her.

The moon's light streams through the trees, and you can

see the owls sitting on their branches. All of a sudden, the owls start to hoot as though to say welcome to you. Perhaps you would like to hoot back so they know you have heard and understood them.

Listen, can you hear the call of the nightingale? The nightingale sings the most beautiful music and only special people like yourself can hear her call. The music is surrounding you, making you feel as though you have entered an enchanted garden, a part of your own garden that you have not been to before.

If you listen carefully, you will hear the sound of water falling. Go further down your pathway, observing the smaller bushes under which some animals are sleeping, until you reach a curve in the pathway. When you go around this curve, you will come to a glorious waterfall streaming down from a great height. Its water is splashing high into the air, catching the moon's light so that its drops appear like crystals of many different colors.

There are rocks surrounding the waterfall, and the water as it lands swirls around these rocks, before passing down into the river that flows from the waterfall further into your garden. Why don't you sit and watch the waterfall with the moon's light highlighting the water, the drops of water like gems being thrown this way and that?

Listen quietly and see if you can hear anything else, apart from the sound of the water falling, or if you can feel something different. Be patient and wait, watching the water all the time while you wait to see what else is going to happen. Put your hand out to catch a stray moonbeam that is making its way toward you, and then look into the palm of your hand.

You have captured a Moonbeam Fairy. She is very beautiful and is standing on your palm, smiling at you, waving her wings in welcome. She is so tiny and everything about her seems magical. Her wings are golden, and her dress glows and shimmers as it is made out of threads that come from the moon's light. Even though she is so tiny and the sound of the waterfall so loud, you can understand her perfectly well.

She wants to take you to a special place. Listen to her, and follow her as she flies in front of you. She is taking you away from the rocks and the waterfall, but not very far, as these rocks and the waterfall are themselves magical. Near the waterfall is a large wishing well made of huge stone rocks. It has a large bucket hanging from a beam across its top, and the water inside this wishing well has come from the magical waterfall.

The waters inside this wishing well are also magical. The Moonbeam Fairy is showing you how to put your wishes into the bucket and then how to lower the bucket into the marvelous waters below. Then your wishes can be absorbed into its waters.

Take your time putting your wishes in, as there are so many things you could wish for. You can always return at another time to put in other wishes, so there is no need to worry that you will not get all your wishes into the bucket.

I wonder what you would like to wish for? You may have to think for a time before lowering the bucket. There are so many things you may like to have for yourself, or you may like to make good wishes for other people, like your family or friends.

The Moonbeam Fairy is laughing as she splashes you with some of the magical waters from the bucket. The waters make you laugh too and feel good inside.

This wishing well will always be there for you whenever you want to return to it. And when you do, the Moonbeam Fairy will come back down upon a ray of the moon's light to welcome you …

The Plane and the Parachute

THE SUN is pouring a lovely golden glow upon your garden that encourages the plants to grow and to reach further upward toward its light.

The blue sky is reflected in the waters of the lakes and streams, and the white clouds balloon, making figures and faces in some parts of the sky, while in others wisps of clouds move quietly across its blue depth.

As you go further forward into your garden, you will

come to a small runway that aircraft use. Sitting on this runway is a silver plane that reflects the sun's light and shines as though it has been polished carefully by hand.

The pilot is beckoning you to come closer. She would like you to enter the plane and to take off into the blue skies with her.

The cabin of the aircraft is beautifully appointed, and the woodwork is polished to a high sheen. The seats are large and lean back when the button on the arm is pushed, so that your feet come off the floor. If you push another button, a small television set will appear in front of you with many more channels than you would normally receive.

The channel you are watching is giving the weather forecast and reports that the conditions for flying are excellent. The cabin steward is coming forward and asking if you would like something to eat or drink, after the plane has taken off. The kitchen has many delights to offer; you can ask for anything you like and it will be brought to you.

The engines are revving up and the plane moves slightly forward, the motor turning over gently. As the plane moves down the runway, the noise from the engines is getting louder and louder, and you can feel the thrust of the plane as it lifts off the runway and into the air—and you are now airborne.

You are moving quickly through the air, with the earth rapidly disappearing beneath you, going higher and higher into the clouds until you are above them. How bright the sky is when you are above the clouds and unable to see the earth below.

There is a parachute underneath your seat. The steward will help to strap it on if you like. It is fairly large and bulky but it also feels comfortable and light. I wonder what it would be like to step out of the plane door and to allow yourself to free-fall, going through those clouds immediately below you, feeling their texture as you part them to pass through. And then to pull the ring of your parachute and to have it blossom forth, allowing you to drift slowly to earth, swaying slightly with the breeze. Would you like to try it? Step out the door and into the air, falling through its freshness and feeling as though you are part of the sky itself.

The plane is circling overhead and the pilot and steward are waving to you. You could give them a wave as your parachute takes you down toward the earth, through the clouds that have shielded the earth from your view, pulling you slightly this way and that, before you land in your special garden near the landing strip.

The plane is coming back in to land. Perhaps you would like to do this all over again, or you may like to ask the pilot if she will show you how to fly the plane itself …

Snorkeling

YOUR GARDEN has so many lovely aromas coming around you from the multitude of flowers that peek up from the earth. Some of these flowers appear to be a little shy and hide near the thick bushes, while others stand tall and erect, proudly showing their faces to the sun.

The sky is so blue and clear, with not a cloud in sight. The warmth of the sun radiates toward earth and to where you are in your garden. You can feel its gentle heat surrounding you.

You can hear the sound of waves coming from a little way off as you walk down your garden pathway. Keep walking forward and you will come to a bend in your pathway. When you turn this bend, you can see before you the sea. It is so large that you wonder how far beyond the skyline it must reach.

The sand is golden and gleams as the sun's rays beam down, and the green waves coming in dance with its light. The waves are gathering momentum further out to sea, and then come crashing into shore, their huge white crests being flattened and turning into small streams that creep silently down the sand.

Why don't you go swimming for a while, allowing the waves to take you to and fro, in and out, up and down? It is fun to be bounced around and to have the water supporting the weight of your body.

But what is that sitting on a mound of sand? Why, it is a

snorkel. If you put it on, you could then go underneath the waves to see what is below the water's surface that you have been playing on.

Down and down you go, deep into the waters. At first you are so pleased to be under the waves that you may not notice the small fish swimming by. But then you do. There are fish of many beautiful colors, and some that you have never seen before. Their colors gleam as the sun's light penetrates the waters and catches them, turning them into an ever-changing scene of color. There are also eels and crayfish, and even some sharks who float lazily past you.

If you go deeper, you will come to a coral reef. This coral forms patterns and is alive in the water; its colors are a moving kaleidoscope. Swimming around and through the coral are many tropical fish that are only seen around these coral reefs. Together, the color of the coral and the fish make a magical paradise like nothing you have seen before.

You may wish to swim further afield with your snorkel or you may decide to return to the shore for a time to rest on the golden sand.

Or perhaps you will decide to return to the coral and its many treasures …

The Monkeys and the Zebras

LISTEN CAREFULLY as you enter your garden. It is very quiet. In the beautiful blue sky, the sun is sending down its gentle rays and there are small clouds floating past, catching the sun's light.

What can you hear? I hear movement in the bushes and I think you should go over there, but be very, very quiet, as you don't want to disturb or frighten whoever it might be. Peek through the bushes now and you will find a small monkey looking back at you. She is darting away to where her family is swinging from tree to tree, chattering to each other as they go. She is beckoning you to follow.

The monkeys are very agile as they move up and down the tree, some hanging from the tree's branches and others skittering along quickly. And some of them are carefully looking at the fur of other monkeys, taking out any dirt they find so that their fur is nice and clean.

I am sure you can swing into the trees and sit on a branch with these monkeys if you would like. Look, the small monkey you saw in the bushes is coming over and is going to sit on your lap. She is calling to the others as she puts her arm around your neck. She is telling them it is quite safe to approach you.

There are other little ones coming closer and closer to you. They are a little shy about being so close, but some would like to become closer and are carrying ripe, golden bananas to share with you. Perhaps you would like to take one of these bananas and share their meal with them.

But I can now hear something else approaching from a distance. Listen . . . What do you hear? The sounds are now coming directly from below where you are sitting on the branch. You see more zebras than you can count coming to rest underneath the tree's branches, taking shelter after having come such a long way. Aren't they beautiful with their bold black and white stripes?

One of the smaller monkeys is climbing down the trunk of the tree and approaching them. Why don't you follow? As you climb down you notice a small zebra. You walk across to it and place your hand gently on its nose. It feels smooth to the touch and slightly damp around the area of the nostril.

The zebra is tossing its head and mane and is now putting its head down to graze the grass. Some of the others are laying on the earth, resting. You could go and lay down with them, resting your head gently against the belly of one of the zebras, possibly even the largest.

The monkeys in the tree are becoming more curious as they watch you and the small monkey on the ground, and they too are coming down to investigate.

Perhaps you could place the small monkey on your shoulder and slide onto the back of the zebra you have been resting against. The zebra is now getting to its feet, shaking its head to and fro as it walks forward, preparing to canter. The monkey is chattering in your ear as the zebra's hooves thud on the earth and you feel the rush of the air as you go forward.

Perhaps you can get the zebra to swerve around and head back to where the rest of the herd and the monkeys are waiting, or perhaps you want to ride and ride, feeling the air moving through your hair and around your body, knowing how safe and secure you are on the zebra's back …

The Sun and the Sun Vehicle

THE LIGHT from the sun shines brightly as you enter your garden, and the animals are lying on the soft earth, feeling the sun's warmth penetrating their skin, making them feel good inside. The trees rise high in the air, their branches reaching as though to touch the blue velvet of the sky above. Small clouds move overhead, drifting, some merging with others to make larger cloud formations.

Look toward the sky and you will notice a large white

bird coming in to land. It is very beautiful and it has landed at your feet. You may like to put your hand out toward the bird, carefully so as not to frighten it, and then pat its feathers, brushing them lightly with your palm. This bird has come to take you high into the heavens above your special garden. Settle yourself comfortably on the bird's feathered back, placing your hands gently on its neck as the bird takes off, soaring upward, away from the earth. Look below and you will see the hills and valleys, and the waterways winding through the lush greenery, with the occasional house nestling nearby. You may even see some farm animals sleeping, enveloped in the sun's rays.

The bird is taking you ever upward, further away from the earth than you have been before, flying in a direct line with the sun and its light. It is now landing on a large cloud and a sun vehicle is waiting for you to board so that you can reach the sun in total comfort.

The sun vehicle is large and golden, and glows with light

and energy that has come from the sun's source. It is shaped like a swan and the swan's neck moves gracefully from side to side, as you glide forward. Your seat is padded with the purest gold fabric and the swan vehicle is adorned with small suns that glow and change color—from a burnished gold to a bright, sunny gold, and then back again, ever changing.

The swan is taking you so close to the sun that you can see the rich texture of its surface glowing like a golden furnace, beaming its rays down to the earth far below. You are being taken around the sun in an arc, so that you can see all aspects of its beauty and you can feel the warmth that is radiating out toward you. This warmth is very gentle and enters you body, making you feel good inside. Your sun vehicle is taking you to the back of the sun and is coming in to land, very softly. As you disembark, you notice that the ground beneath your feet and the air surrounding you have a warmth not much different from that which you experience at home. The sun people modify the light that comes from the sun so that those who visit them are comfortable within its light.

There is a sun lady coming forward to greet you and to take you by the hand. Her dress is made of the finest gossamer and floats as she moves. She has a large golden sun over her forehead that sends out light all around her. She is holding out her hand toward you. You feel very secure taking her hand and you understand her speech pattern, which is that of the sun gods.

She is now taking you through a small door. The knob is made of golden mesh and the door itself has emblems etched that show the sun at its many stages of light. The corridor is lit with miniature suns placed along the walls. The drawings on the walls show not only the sun that you are currently visiting, but other suns and other moons and other universes.

The Sun Lady is taking you into a room that has sun people who have been waiting for your arrival. They are going to show you how to reach these other suns, moons, and universes. Why don't you listen to them and learn how to travel to these other places? You may like to visit them at some time in the future.

Take your time with these sun people and when you are ready to return to your special garden, your swan sun vehicle will transport you back to where you belong …

The Ant, the Grasshopper, and the Purple Bird

THE GRANDFATHER Tree is waving his branches at you in welcome. The light breeze rustles through the many leaves on his broad and strong branches, and they appear to dance as the sun's light dapples through them.

Parthia, the purple bird, has come to perch on one of his lower branches, digging her brilliant yellow claws into the wood for support. The blue feathers on the crest of her head move slightly and stand out against the purple of the rest of her body.

There are many animals coming forward to gather around the Grandfather Tree. His wide, leafy branches give them shade and they love to rest nearby, close to his trunk.

Coming down the pathway are two small figures carrying musical instruments that are nearly as big as they are. Why, it is an ant and a grasshopper. They are coming quickly over the grass and the leaves that lay there, and the animals make noises of welcome, each in their own way. The lions roar, the monkeys chatter, and the giraffes throw their long necks around in laughter at the sight of these two small musicians.

The ant and the grasshopper have reached the base of the Grandfather Tree and are placing their instruments against his trunk as they greet the animals that have gathered there. Perhaps you would like to join them and lean against the Grandfather Tree's sturdy trunk, feeling his energy and strength.

The ant and the grasshopper are going to play a lively tune for you and then perhaps a lullaby. The cello is higher than the ant, but he stands tall and reaches the strings, plucking at them and bringing forth a beautiful sound. The grasshopper has a very old battered violin, but the music that pours forth seems as though it is made of magic. The ant and the grasshopper, each with their own bow, bend in time to the rhythm, as they bring forth music such as you have never heard.

Parthia, sitting on one of the Grandfather Tree's lower branches, begins to sing, her beautiful voice harmonizing with the music that comes from the cello and the violin. The music makes you want to dance. Why don't you move nearer to the musicians and allow yourself to feel the music flowing through your veins, your body, your heart, your mind, and . . . dance!

Because Parthia sings so beautifully, you may even decide to sing with her. You could either join her on her branch, or lean against the trunk of this wise old tree. You will find the music that the ant and the grasshopper bring forth from the cello and the violin vibrates through your garden. The flowers sway in tune with the music, while the bushes shake their sturdy bodies and the trees seem to dance. Parthia sings on and her voice, the cello, and the violin seem as one as the music echoes around you.

The ant is offering you the cello. Perhaps you would like to pluck the strings to see what sound you can bring forth. If you would prefer to play the violin, I am sure the grasshopper will allow you to do so.

I am sure that the music you play shall be very special to all who hear it, and perhaps you may even make up your own tunes that will live in the hearts of those who hear them forever …

The Toys' House

THERE IS an air of excitement as you enter your special garden, a feeling as though something is about to happen. I wonder what it can be? The animals are coming forward to greet you as they always do, and several small colorful birds are landing on your shoulders as you go down your garden path. The air is crisp and fresh, and the flowers are preening themselves in all their beautiful colors.

The Grandfather Tree is waving his branches at you and

birds take into the air as he does so, swirling around and making sounds of greeting. Why don't you go over to the old tree, who seems as though he has lived forever, to see what all this excitement is about?

What is that under the shade of the Grandfather Tree? Why, it is the largest toys' house you have ever seen. It is filled with toys of all descriptions. Although it is large, you are still a little too big to fit inside. Why don't you see yourself becoming smaller and smaller, until you are just the right size to fit?

Now that you are small, why don't you go inside? The front door is painted red and the handle a bright yellow. You can hear sounds from inside as you turn the handle. I wonder what they are? As you open the door and step inside, many voices call out, "Surprise, surprise." All the toys have gathered to greet you as you enter.

There are many, many teddy bears, each of them looking quite different from the others. Some of them have hats and vests on, some are twirling their canes, and some are looking after the small bears who are bouncing around with glee at your look of surprise on finding them.

There are beautiful dolls dressed in their best clothes. Some stand tall and proud, and others sit in comfortable chairs. Many of them come from other countries and are dressed in their national costumes. I wonder if you can recognize where they come from? If you cannot, just ask them as they would love to tell you about their homes. Some of them are gypsies. If you look out the back window, you will see their caravans and horses parked outside, all of them wearing garlands of flowers around their necks.

The trolls are laughing as they tumble over each other to reach you. These are the lucky trolls that normally live in the valleys, hidden away from sight from most people, but not from you.

There are many toy animals that have come to life. Oh

look, here comes a baby elephant with his long ears swinging from side to side. And there are a tiger and a lion, both growling softly in welcome.

There is a stairway that will take you to the next level, where you will find all sorts of other toys and books. Some of the books are open on the tables as though they have just been read, and the beds look comfortable enough to jump into.

Why don't you investigate each level of the toys' house to see what else you can find? There are so many treasures and toys that live here, that you may not be able to see them all at once. See what you can for now, and remember that you can always return another time to see and find the treasures and toys you have not seen this time …

The Clock

THE AIR in your special garden is fresh, with a light breeze touching your cheek, and the sun is beaming down upon you. The green grass is like a soft carpet underneath your feet, and the huge trees with their spreading branches are protecting the smaller plants that grow nearby. In the sky are many small clouds floating silently above, and the birds are calling to each other.

Your pathway winds in front of you, and, as you follow it,

you will come to a large building. It is a very unusual building with many turrets, and at the top of these turrets are the faces of different clocks. If you look at the building itself, it is made in the shape of a clock. Can you hear it ticking? Tick tock, tick tock. The sound is really quite loud.

One of the hands from the face of this clock building is coming down to pick you up. You feel very safe and secure as it lifts you high into the air. It seems funny to be transported in this way, swinging through the air until you come face to face with the clock itself.

The clock has eyes with long eyelashes and it is blinking at you. It also has a wide mouth that is smiling. I think this clock has been waiting for you to come and wants you to enter through the door hidden in its left ear. Open the door and you will see a winding stairway that will take you deep inside the workings of the clock.

Luckily the inside of the clock building is insulated so

that the sound of the workings isn't too loud for those who work within it. The clock people are working on the second hands to ensure that the clock keeps exactly on time. Why don't you go closer so that you can see how they work? The clock people would love to explain what they do and to show you the inner workings of the clock.

Now you may like to go upstairs so that you can enter some of the turret clocks and see how they work. The people who look after these clocks love to have people visit them and to show them not only how the insides of these clocks move, but how they are all tuned together to be always at the same time.

If you want, you can alter these clocks so that they all tell different times or have different chimes. For instance, you could have the clock facing west show a different time from the southern one, or you could make the big clock that controls the building have a much louder, or different sounding, chime. All the clocks could strike the hour at different times and with different chimes.

Having these different chimes pealing forth could be quite musical. You could adjust the chimes yet again to get a different tune going across the fields and into the townships.

Or you could have these clocks putting on a show on the hour and the half hour, with doors opening and closing on the clock faces, and with a small theatre inside where a show goes on and entertains those who watch. You could become involved in what type of theatre will appear on the hour and the half hour. I wonder what story you will choose to tell …

Mr. and Mrs. Santa Claus

YOUR GARDEN has been transformed into a Winter Wonderland full of huge fir trees, their branches laden with sparkling white snow. If you listen carefully, you will hear the tinkle of bells as the reindeer come closer and closer to where you are standing. Their sleigh is red and glows in the sun's gentle light, and there is a blanket folded on the seat, waiting for someone to place it over their knees when they sit on the golden seat.

Why don't you sit in the sleigh and allow the reindeer to

take you to their home? It isn't very far to go and the bells on the sleigh ring out as the reindeer make their way through the trees, traveling quickly across through the deep snow.

They are pulling up near a small yellow house that has smoke coming out from several chimneys. A man dressed in a red suit with white fur trim is standing at the front door to greet you. I wonder if you can recognize who it is?

Santa Claus is so happy that you have come to visit. He is wondering if you would like to help prepare the Christmas presents. Sometimes it is very difficult for Santa Claus and Mrs. Claus to make toys for all the children in the world. Each year there are more and more children writing and saying what they most want for Christmas.

Why don't you put on a Santa suit or a Mrs. Claus suit and then you can become a Santa helper? There are many suits there to choose from. Select the one that is just the right size for you and put it on. As you do so, if you have chosen a Santa

Claus suit you will notice that you feel thicker around the belly and you want to laugh. Send the laugh out and you will hear it echoing around the room, just as Santa's laugh does. If you have chosen a Mrs. Claus suit, you may feel you want to bustle around and take care of everyone, just like she does.

Some Santa helpers go in the sleigh and help to distribute toys to the children. And some have to climb down the chimney! I wonder if you will fit? Wouldn't that be fun, to climb down and put the presents into the stockings that hang over the fireplace? Not everyone has a fireplace of course, but Santa always knows how to creep into the bedroom when the children are fast asleep, placing the presents at the foot of the bed. Or he may put the presents at the base of the Christmas tree, which sometimes has fairy lights blinking. In any case, the children receive a lovely surprise when they open their eyes and leap out from their bed on Christmas morning.

Mrs. Claus is always busy and she helps Santa in many

ways. She and the elves work together to get the toys finished in time and she seems to have a never-ending flow of food arriving for the workers. The elves whistle while they work, and Mrs. Claus smiles and sings along with them. Perhaps you may prefer to stay with Mrs. Claus and the elves. You too could make some toys or perhaps dress some dolls, putting a big bow in their hair and painting a large smile on their faces.

Mr. and Mrs. Claus love having children help them out at this special time of the year. It doesn't matter what you choose to do, whether you want to be a smaller Santa or Mrs. Claus, or even if you decide to become an elf, which also would be fun.

If you decide to be an elf, your costume will be green, your shoes will curl up at the toes and you will have a bright red buckle. You will have a small hat with a feather sitting perkily on your head.

Perhaps this time you could be Mr. Claus, and next time Mrs. Claus or an elf. It is always up to you …

The Green Frog and the Castle

THE LEAVES from the many trees are rustling in the light breeze that has entered your garden, moving them gently. The sound of water falling drifts toward you, making you feel you would like to see where this sound comes from. Your garden path is lined with green bushes whose yellow flowers are preening themselves to catch the gentle warmth of the sun. If you follow this path, you will come to a large waterfall whose spray is being thrown high into the air. The light catches the droplets, turning them into colored gems as they turn in the air, before landing and being absorbed into the earth.

Nearby there is a small pond that is untouched by the waterfall and its rainbow of drops. This pond is quiet and tranquil, and the sound from the waterfall is like music as it drifts across its still waters. There are many lily pads on the pond, and sitting on one of the larger ones is a frog.

This green frog has large eyes that seem to see everything as he sits on the lily pad. He hops from one lily pad to another, coming closer to you all the time. He may be a little shy. Why don't you smile and beckon him over? Now he is hopping more quickly than before and his large mouth is turned up in a big smile. He is coming closer to where you are standing and, with a final hop, there he is in front of you.

He has a floppy, golden velvet hat on his head. There is a large bow sitting on the left-hand side made out of green silk, which has small suns and moons embroidered on it. There are four golden buttons holding his waistcoat together that look like small stars, and the waistcoat itself is shiny and gleams in the sun's light, its reds and purples glowing. The cane he is holding is made of gold and the top has a large emblem embellished with rubies.

He is tapping his cane and his large feet move in time to the music it makes. Why don't you move the way he does? He is dancing along the pathway, enjoying the sun's light as it dapples through the trees. He is taking you down the pathway to a small hill. In the side of this hill is a castle. The frog is using his cane to press the doorbell and, as the chimes ring out, you can hear excited voices from inside, "It's Mr. Frog, it's Mr. Frog, and he has brought someone with him."

A lady with long golden hair opens the door for you to enter, and behind her are her children. Some of these children also have blonde hair, while others have bright red hair. Mr. Frog takes his hat off and hands it to you. It feels lovely and soft. Perhaps you would like to put it on. Some of the children are laughing as you do so, and they want to try the hat on too.

The castle is large, and has high ceilings and a staircase that is both very wide and long. The children would like you to go upstairs with them before dinner is served. They want to show you their rooms and how they live. Why don't you go with them? It would be such fun to explore a castle, to see what the large rooms and turrets hold. It would be such an adventure going into each room and turret. I am sure each one is full of surprises.

Mr. Frog and the lady of the castle will wait for you to return. They have arranged an elaborate supper for you, as you may be hungry when you return. Take your time looking around with the children and return when you are ready …

The Magic Cloak

THE FRESHNESS of the air caresses your skin as you walk down your garden path, and the flowers in their prettiest colors peek out at you as if to say "Hello." The trees reach with their branches high into the sky, and their green leaves shine in the light coming from the golden sun.

The animals are coming forward to greet you, as they always do, and many birds are coming to perch upon the branches of the trees and are calling to you. The butterflies fly around you, touching you gently with their wings, and some settle upon your hair and shoulders. The small rabbits are hopping past as though they have somewhere special to go, while others are popping their heads out of their burrows to see what is happening.

Your garden has a feeling of magic, of mystery. The air itself seems different and the aroma from the flowers is more pungent than normal. You feel as though you are being enveloped by this aroma, almost as though it has formed a cloak around you that no one else can see—but you can not only see it, you can also feel it.

This is a magic cloak that can take you anywhere you want. Because no one else can see it except you, when it surrounds you, you become invisible to all. Being invisible can be such fun. You can wander through your garden, looking at everything around you, and the animals will sense that you are there but wonder why they cannot see you.

Where would you like to go in your magic cloak? You can be transported to any place you want. You may even want to start first of all with being at home and seeing how it feels to stand behind your mother and father, or perhaps one of your friends, and place your hand upon their waist. I am sure they will feel your touch and turn around, wondering where you are and why they felt you touch them. If you laugh, they will hear your laughter and assume you are playing hide and seek with them, and then they will try to find you.

Your magic cloak can take you to other countries, to places you have not been before. I wonder where you would like to go?

You may want to travel to the sun and to see how the sun sends its light down to the earth, illuminating the houses, the trees and the flowers, and helping all that live on the earth to grow by feeling its warmth and energy.

Or you may want to go to the moon just to see if a man

really does live there as people say, and also to find out what is on the other side of the moon.

If you find you do go to the sun or the moon, and you meet the sun gods and the moon goddesses, then do take your cloak off so that they can see you. They will then take you to all parts of the sun and moon so that you can have as many lovely experiences as you would like.

You may decide to visit Japan and to see how the Japanese live. Their buildings are so different from ours and so is their traditional clothing. They have lovely tea ceremonies and I am sure you would be invited to join them if you let them know you were there.

Perhaps you may want to go to Africa and to see the lovely African people who look after their land and the amazing animals that live there. Many of the animals in Africa cannot be found anywhere else in the world, except in zoos. Again, take off your magic cloak so they know you are there, and perhaps you can ride one of the giraffes or elephants, or swim in the waterhole with the hippopotamuses.

Your beautiful magic cloak will take you so easily and carefully to wherever you want to go. You cannot lose it. No matter where you put it down and where you go, when you want to return the cloak is always there for you to put back on.

When you are ready to go back to your special garden, put your cloak back on and return. Place the magic cloak at the base of the Grandfather Tree's trunk so that you know where to find it when next you want it …

The Mauve Fairy

THERE ARE many tulips raising their heads to the sun's light as you enter your garden, and their various colors glow and pulsate within its warmth. There are several small birds sitting on the branches of the smaller bushes. The sound of their voices blends harmoniously with the sound of the bees as they go about their busy work of taking the pollen from the glorious flowers that abound in your special garden.

The Grandfather Tree stands tall and serene, spreading

his enormous branches to cover the smaller plants that need the shade, and also the animals that like to rest near his large roots. Many colorful birds have come to rest upon these branches, as have some of the owls that you hear at night.

The Grandfather Tree is moving one of his large branches as though he wants you to look at something. Because this branch is high up, you will need to climb his thick trunk. You find this easy to do, as small stairs appear that help you make your way up the trunk. As you step up each stair they return into the tree so that no one else can follow. Walk along the sturdy branch that the Grandfather Tree has been waving and, when you get to the center where the leaves are the thickest, sit down and part the leaves to see what is inside.

Why, it is a fairy! And one who is so pretty. Her delicate mauve dress floats easily through the air, and her silver wings gleam in the sun's light. Her wand is also silver, and when she touches you with it, you too sprout wings like hers. But your wings are golden, your clothes become a beautiful apricot color, and you too have a wand that matches your wings.

The fairy is fluttering her wings to show you how they move. Start to move your own wings now, and you will lift up into the air with the mauve fairy and hover there for a short time with her. The Grandfather Tree is shaking his branches with laughter and pleasure, as he knew you would like to become a fairy and fly. The owls are opening their eyes wide, and the small colorful birds are lifting off into the air, fluttering their wings just like you.

You feel happy flying with the mauve fairy, and your wings move easily, taking you through the fresh air. Whenever you want to land, your wings slow down and you will hover above the flower or bush you want to land on, and then gently your feet will come down.

The mauve fairy is taking you through different parts of your special garden, introducing you to the nature spirits who look after the flowers, the bushes, and the trees. Each flower, each bush, and each tree, has its own nature spirits who care for it and love it. Nature spirits are normally a little shy and hide themselves, but because the mauve fairy is taking you to meet them, they are friendly and happy to be with you.

The mauve fairy is now taking you deeper and deeper within your garden, to an area you have not been to before. You can see small fairy lights lighting the way beneath you, as though they have been strung through the trees and bushes, and you can hear the music of small violins, harps, and cellos. You are being taken into the fairy kingdom where all the fairies return when their work has been done. There they can rest and play and dance to the music, which is so lovely.

Because you have come with your friend, the mauve fairy, all the other fairies are welcoming you and wanting you to stay with them. They are dressed beautifully, as you are, but in so many different colors. Their wings gleam in the light from the sun, which is sometimes hiding behind small clouds that drift past.

The fairies are asking you to stay with them for as long as you like. They are about to sit at their toadstools and eat, while some of their friends entertain them with music and dancing. Why don't you join them? You can eat fairy bread, and tiny fairy cakes, and other unusual foods they have.

You may even want to get up and dance with the fairies later on. If so, join them and feel the music coursing through your veins, knowing there is no right or wrong way to dance, because the music itself will move your body.

Stay with these fairies as long as you like, and when you need to return to the Grandfather Tree, your friend the mauve fairy will fly back with you to his wide, comfortable branches …